HAIKU TO NURSE BY

Haiku to Nurse By

MELANIE S. LEWIS

Dear Zoe!
In celebration
of friendship & family!
All my love,
Melanie

SMALL BATCH BOOKS
AMHERST, MASSACHUSETTS

Designed by Megan Katsanevakis

Cover art by Katie m. Berggren

Author photo by dani. fine photography

Library of Congress Control Number: 2018940129

ISBN: 9780982975886

SMALL
BATCH
BOOKS

493 SOUTH PLEASANT STREET
AMHERST, MASSACHUSETTS 01002
413.230.3943
SMALLBATCHBOOKS.COM

For Madison and Perry

Contents

Preface

THIS BOOK is a collection of whimsical verse modeled after the beautiful and delicate structure of Japanese haiku.

The tiny word clusters you will find on the following pages formed in my mind in these rhythmic patterns almost unintentionally. Sometimes I wonder if poetry is as instinctual and universal as drawing breath: We think, therefore we write in verse.

My children were my prompts. Their expressions, gestures, and personalities, and the joys and heartaches of parenting—and of life—were my inspiration. These poems fell out onto the page like a collage, in layers of images and experiences. Over the years, with the passage of time and much reflection, poems have been added, rewritten, and fine-tuned. Finally, each one bears a neatly tailored resemblance to precious and poignant snapshots in time. They are informal haiku, wrapped in a mixture of silliness and sentiment.

Each poem captures a true memory and is meant to entertain, console, and share fellowship and camaraderie with anyone and everyone who, like me, has experienced the wonder and awe of infants and children, which plows the way to carry us through.

-Melanie S. Lewis

$\mathcal{O}ne$

LET THE GAMES BEGIN

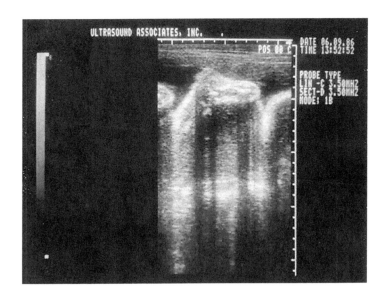

A footprint on the
screen is the beginning of
his grand adventures.

Bones cramp hot and cold
to tear open a safe place
for baby's first breath.

He lay under lights
naked butt high in the air—
bilirubin counts.

Nine fourteen and a
half at birth after he peed.
Truth is he weighed ten.

The only time I
write is at night while rocking
my sweet boy to sleep.

Two

THERE IS NO FORMULA FOR THIS

Nursing every two
hours, every two hours,
every two hours.

Rude awakenings . . .
breasts like rocks and wet t-shirts
before the dawn breaks.

For nursing mothers
the sound of baby crying
is a hard letdown.

Hear the gentle drone
the lullaby baby knows
electric breast pumps.

She lifts and tugs for
breast milk here, there, everywhere
no more modesty.

Breastfed babies learn
earlier to count to two
than babes on bottles.

My hair is flowing
gracefully, quietly down
the bath drain in clumps.

To choose one's clothing
one must carefully decide
what will hide the leaks.

Baby is content
nursing quietly until
attention shifts—*"OUCH!"*

So soft and supple
she can nurse while watching her
cat across the room.

Another fine use
for a paper towel is
breast pad on the run.

Don't worry if love-
making is stimulating
for areolae.

I chatted with friends
while nursing you but stopped when
I saw you judging.

My milk strengthens you.
My milk soothes you to sleep. My
milk is our shared breath.

Lying on pillows
she sips, we rest, eyes soaking
up each other's souls.

Three

NIGHT-NIGHT, MY SWEET

In the dark hours
I fumble with wet diapers
and too many snaps.

Feel and remember
how he softly touched your face
just before he slept.

After rocking and
nursing and pacing and prayer
she finally sleeps.

Sudden screams wake us
in a startle, running, dazed
slapped out of a dream.

His night terrors gripped
me. The blessing was that he
never remembered.

The mobile hangs down
black and white; its slow, soft spins
share lines with her smiles.

The doubt and worry
fall away like rain as I
watch my baby sleep.

Four

BABIES ON A MISSION

Even while wrapped in
a snowsuit the power of
his will bores straight through.

I tried to tuck him
in his crib all cozy warm
but each time he fled.

She reaches out hard
on the edge of falling hard
to touch a dried leaf.

The nurse could not hold
him still to draw blood. She paused,
shocked and bewildered.

I reached down to get
a baby wipe and *CRASH!* He
rolled off to find me.

They push away and
run. Nurture independence.
That is my mantra.

He leaps far beyond
milestones. It's no wonder—
early-onset gray.

Already she stands
while holding my fingers tight
balancing her joy.

Five

CHARTING GROWTH

A thoughtful pose with
finger to forehead scratching
is just cradle cap.

He rolls left, creeps right
repeating movements over
with each success, more.

How does she know how
to use one small fingertip
to brush off a crumb?

She's starting to string
more and more words together
like "cookie," "more," "please."

You can't imagine
a parent's pride when baby
learns to blow her nose.

Toe to toe, pinky
to nose, my little one's growth
is measured in clothes.

Mommy, wawa, juice,
kitty, birdie, baby, tree,
doggie, cheese, moon, *ME!*

The hearing exam:
"Place pegs in holes." But my son
created patterns.

His abstract thinking
caused shock and awe among all
of kindergarten.

Our separation
began with her first bottle
and her first two teeth.

She leans and cuddles
against my cheek still but soon
she'll stand without me.

Six

ANXIETY AND AWE

I was a nervous
new mother, ringing the nurse
for a simple sneeze.

Bathtub splashing and
giggles, a ritual we
protect gleefully.

When my baby girl
rests her head on my shoulder
nothing else matters.

For hours and years
he rubbed my thumbnail, it seemed
it gave him comfort.

That blond shock of hair,
the birthmark that let me know
I'd always find him.

Ignoring her tears
is as impossible as
writing without words.

Ear infections slip
in at night. We rejoice at
dawn when fevers break.

It is Mother's Day,
a pruning and planting day
for playing in dirt.

Two hundred dollars
for a cardboard box with holes.
The toy costs extra.

Whisper in her ear
she'll know your voice, your smell, your
words are her focus.

The only time I
write is at night while rocking
my sweet girl to sleep.

Seven

SHOW AND TELL WHO YOU ARE

Perfect little boy.
Quick and agile in mind and
body. My treasure.

Her morning chatter
to Grover, Bunny, and Pooh
wakes me with giggles.

Always on the move
he could run sprints at nine months,
athletic genius.

Nicknames from strangers:
Refrigerator Perry.
Also, Fabio.

A toddler who could
throw a perfect overhand.
Pitching to the mitt.

Her bright energy
leads me out of the darkness
and fills me with light.

Never did he have
a tantrum. He was stoic
to a fault, always.

Is it a sign when
your newborn's muscles are etched,
defined like marble?

She seemed picky for
plain pasta and bananas
but she craved garlic.

Celebrate the moon
with baby on your knee where
she greets the angels.

Eight

BROTHER AND SISTER

His invisible
friends were Brother and Sister
so I took the hint.

She's such a mother—
as soon as the meal is served
she runs for Brother.

When baby is nine
months and brother is ten years
he looks college-bound.

All her body shakes
giggling from inside out.
Brother must be home.

Nine
REMEMBERING DADS

His joy was brightest
with his father. When he leaves,
deep sadness remains.

Dad dreamt he nursed you
last night but today he used
spoonfuls of water.

Your dad did it all
and would have nursed you, too, if
nature had allowed.

Grandfathers travel
back to boyhood when standing
on the baseball field.

Ten

PLAY AND MISCHIEF, MISCHIEF AND PLAY

The piano keys
chip from her wooden mallet.
How she loves music.

She used her potty
as if it were a toy box
until she turned two.

A red pail becomes
a hat. Such silliness in
unexpected things.

When it has handles
a brown paper bag becomes
a little girl's purse.

When he runs to me
head lowered, arms reaching back
my love catches him.

Latch the cupboards and
the gates, the little ones are
loose and on their feet!

My toddler climbs up
with more guts and will than a
fat corporation.

The boys gathered round
her, waiting to receive their
orders, happily.

Eleven

BUBBLES, BUBBLES, BUBBLES

Baby blew bubbles
while bathing in her sink bath
one thumb dipped in soap.

The wide-eyed wonder
when blades of grass do not pop
her fallen bubbles.

Her palm and wet skin
a small, natural cradle
for catching bubbles.

She dips her wand and
twirls, creating soapy worlds,
then blows them kisses.

About the Poet

Melanie S. Lewis was raised on Long Island, in New York. She received her Bachelor of Arts degree from Sarah Lawrence College and her law degree from Western New England University School of Law. She is a litigator and an appellate attorney primarily representing indigent clients in civil and criminal matters.

Lewis raised her children in the Pioneer Valley of Western Massachusetts, where she still lives and works. Her son, Perry, is the owner of Philly Phitness, a personal training gym in Philadelphia. Her daughter, Madison, is a college student studying theater and writing.

Lewis has had individual poems published and has led creative writing workshops for teens and survivors of domestic violence. This is her first book.